Rodeph Sholom School
168 West 79th Street
New York, NY 10024

Native American Biographies

SACAGAWEA

Rachel A. Koestler-Grack

Heinemann Library
Chicago, Illinois

© 2004 Heinemann Library
a division of Reed Elsevier Inc.
Chicago, Illinois

Customer Service   888–454–2279

Visit our website at www.heinemannlibrary.com

Designed by Kim Saar/Heinemann Library
Maps by John Fleck
Photo research by Alan Gottlieb
Printed in China by WKT Company Limited

08 07 06 05 04
10 9 8 7 6 5 4 3 2 1

Library of Congress Cataloging-in-Publication Data
Koestler-Grack, Rachel A., 1973-
  Sacagawea / Rachel A. Koestler-Grack.
    p. cm. -- (Native American biographies)
  Summary: A biography of Sacagawea, describing her childhood, kidnapping by an enemy tribe at age twelve, and service as an interpreter to Lewis and Clark and the Corps of Discovery as they crossed the country to the Pacific Ocean.
  Includes bibliographical references and index.
  ISBN 1-4034-5004-8 (lib. bdg.) -- ISBN 1-4034-5011-0 (pbk.)
  1. Sacagawea--Juvenile literature. 2. Lewis and Clark Expedition (1804-1806)--Juvenile literature. 3. Shoshoni women--Biography--Juvenile literature. [1. Sacagawea. 2. Shoshoni Indians--Biography. 3. Indians of North America--Biography. 4. Women--Biography. 5. Lewis and Clark Expedition (1804-1806)] I. Title. II. Series: Native American biographies (Heinemann Library (Firm))
  F592.7.S123K64 2004
  978.004'974574'0092--dc22
                            2003020492

Acknowledgments
The author and publisher are grateful to the following for permission to reproduce copyright material:
pp. 4, 17 Michael Haynes Historic Art; pp. 5, 25, 27 Clymer Museum of Art; p. 7 Library of Congress/Neg. #LC-USZ62-115466; pp. 8, 12 Macduff Everton/Corbis; p. 10 Smithsonian American Art Museum/Art Resource; p. 11 Illustration by Karen Carr/Lewis and Clark State Historical Site/Illinois Historic Preservation Agency and Illinois Capital Development Board; p. 14 Painting "Lewis and Clark: The Departure from the Wood River Encampment, May 14, 1804" by Gary R. Lucy/Gary R. Lucy Gallery, Inc; pp. 19, 21 Gilcrease Museum; p. 20 Montana Historical Society; p. 23 Western History and Genealogy Department/Denver Public Library; p. Jefferson National Expansion Memorial/National Park Service; p. 28 Connie Ricca/Corbis; p. 29 James Leynse/Corbis SABA

Cover photographs by (foreground) Connie Ricca/Corbis, (background) Corbis

Special thanks to Rod Ariwite for his help in the preparation of this book.

Every effort has been made to contact copyright holders of any material reproduced in this book. Any omissions will be rectified in subsequent printings if notice is given to the publisher.

For more information about the statue of Sacagawea on the cover of this book, turn to page 28.
The background shows a river in the northwestern United States.

Contents

▸ Some words are shown in bold, **like this.** You can
▸ find out what they mean by looking in the glossary.

Seeing the Big Water

Seventeen-year-old Sacagawea sat in a long, narrow boat. She held her son Pomp on her lap. Sacagawea was proud to be a Lemhi Shoshone Indian. For eight months, she had traveled with a group of 31 explorers. It had not been easy to travel over a thousand miles with a baby. The group was led by two explorers: Meriwether Lewis and William Clark. The group was called the **Corps** of Discovery.

This image of Sacagawea was painted by artist Michael Haynes.

The group was traveling to the Pacific Coast. Sacagawea had never seen the ocean before. She was excited to see the "big water." Sacagawea helped the explorers travel safely from present-day North Dakota to Oregon. She helped open the door to the West.

The Corps of Discovery

The Corps of Discovery started in St. Louis, Missouri. Its **mission** was to explore the land along the Missouri River all the way to the Pacific Ocean.

Sacagawea traveled with the Corps of Discovery from present-day North Dakota to the coast of Oregon.

Kidnapped

In 1788 Sacagawea was born in a tepee near present-day Salmon, Idaho. She was part of an important family. Sacagawea's father was the chief of their **tribe**, the Lemhi Shoshone. She had an older brother named Cameahwait, an older sister named Pine Girl, and a younger brother named Snag.

Sacagawea's Name

People disagree on the spelling of Sacagawea's name. Most people use the spelling *Sacagawea*. Others spell her name *Sakakawea*. Many Lemhi Shoshone people use the spelling *Sacajawea*. Her name is usually pronounced *Sah-cah-jah-WEE-ah*.

Sacagawea often played games with friends. On hot, summer days, Sacagawea swam in rivers and streams. Like other Lemhi Shoshone girls, Sacagawea often gathered berries. Sacagawea's mother taught her how to dry fruits and fish. The women of Sacagawea's family also showed her how to make clothes, build tepees, and take care of children. The Lemhi Shoshone people were **nomadic.** They moved often. They followed deer, elk, or buffalo herds. Sacagawea learned to pack and travel for long distances.

This photograph of a Shoshone Indian camp was taken around 1900.

When Sacagawea was twelve, her people camped near the Jefferson River in present-day Montana. One morning, some of the men left the camp to hunt. Sacagawea's brother Cameahwait went with them. Suddenly, a loud war cry came from beyond some trees. A group of **warriors** from the Hidatsa **tribe** was coming. The Shoshone men ran to get their bows and arrows. Sacagawea ran into a nearby forest with the other women and children.

The photograph shows the Jefferson River in Montana. The Jefferson River flows into the Missouri River.

Suddenly Sacagawea was captured by the Hidatsa warriors. As they rode back to the camp, Sacagawea

saw the body of her dead mother. The Hidatsa warriors set the tepees on fire. The warriors left the campsite, taking Sacagawea and several other young girls with them. One of the other prisoners was Sacagawea's good friend, Mountain Sage.

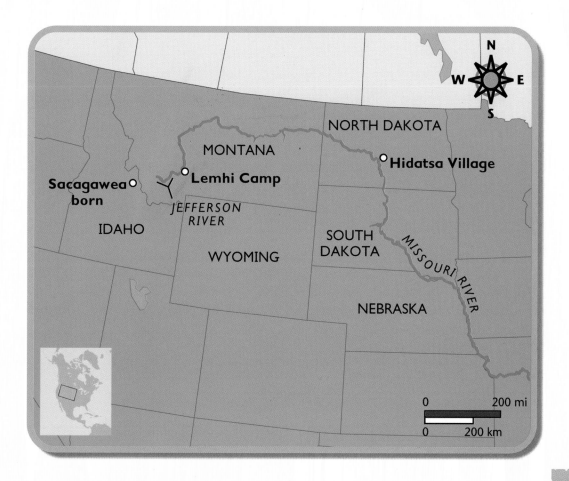

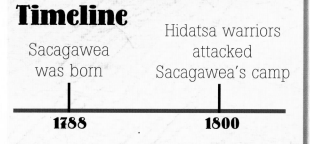

A New Life

Life in the Hidatsa village was different. Sacagawea and Mountain Sage lived with the **warrior** who had captured them. The Hidatsas lived in large, **dome**-shaped houses made from wood, grass, and mud. The girls learned to plant gardens of corn, beans, and squash. They helped the women cook meals and clean buffalo **hides.** Most of the time, the warrior treated Sacagawea like one of his own children.

This painting of a Hidatsa village in present-day North Dakota was made by artist George Catlin. The area is now a national historic site.

*Toussaint Charbonneau was around 47 years old when he and Sacagawea joined the **Corps** of Discovery.*

One day, a French fur trader named Toussaint Charbonneau visited the Hidatsa warrior's house. Charbonneau bought the girls from the warrior. They became his wives. In October of 1804 some white explorers came to the village. They built a camp near the Hidatsa village called Fort Mandan. Day after day, Charbonneau visited Fort Mandan. One morning, Charbonneau told Sacagawea to pack some clothing, food, and blankets. They were going to live in Fort Mandan.

*The **Corps** of Discovery spent the winter at Fort Mandan. The fort was recently **reconstructed.***

Sacagawea met the explorers. The leaders' names were Meriwether Lewis and William Clark. But Sacagawea gave them different names. Lewis always carried a big knife. Sacagawea called him Long Knife. Sacagawea liked the color of Clark's hair. She called him Red Hair.

Lewis and Clark visited the
Hidatsa camp

Sacagawea gave birth to Pomp

1804	**1805**

On February 11, 1805, Sacagawea felt sharp pains in her stomach. Lewis helped her give birth to a baby boy. Charbonneau named the boy Jean Baptiste. But Sacagawea called him *Pomp*—a Lemhi Shoshone word that means "hair." A month later Charbonneau told Sacagawea that they would travel west with the explorers. The explorers wanted them to be **interpreters**.

What Is an Interpreter?

An interpreter **translates** one language into another. Sacagawea would translate the Lemhi Shoshone language into the Hidatsa language for Charbonneau. Charbonneau could then translate the message into English for the explorers.

Beginning the Journey

On April 7, 1805, Sacagawea and Charbonneau met with the explorers on the bank of the Missouri River near Fort Mandan. Sacagawea saw six small boats and two long, narrow sailboats. She was used to riding horses. She probably wondered why the white men would choose to travel by water instead of on horseback.

> The **Corps** of Discovery traveled much of the way to the Pacific Ocean in boats like these.

Lewis and Clark did many things that **puzzled** Sacagawea. They used a compass to help them find their way. Sacagawea's people always used the sun, moon, and stars to guide them. Every night, the men wrote notes in their books. Sacagawea did not know what the men were writing. But she understood that the papers were important.

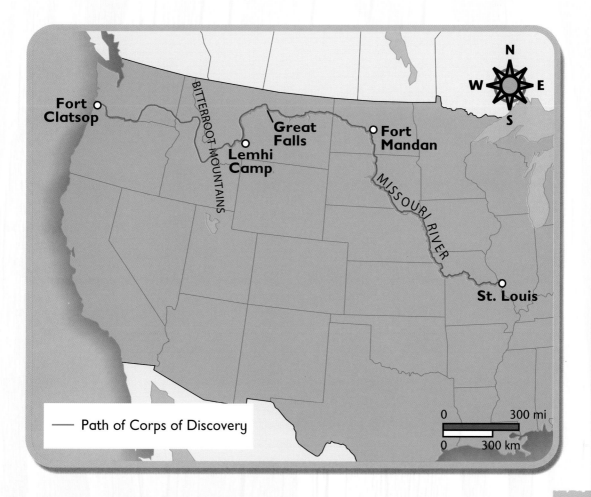

Fort Clatsop

BITTERROOT MOUNTAINS

Great Falls

Lemhi Camp

Fort Mandan

MISSOURI RIVER

St. Louis

N
W E
S

—— Path of Corps of Discovery

0   300 mi
0   300 km

Sacagawea worked hard on the trip. At night the group would set up camp. Sacagawea searched nearby forests for wild roots and berries. One day, danger came to Sacagawea and the men in her boat. While they were traveling, a strong wind caught the boat's sail. The boat tipped. The men tried to get the boat upright. Charbonneau and the other men panicked. But Sacagawea was not scared. She knew how to swim.

In Their Own Words

"The Indian woman . . . caught and [saved] most of the light articles which were washed overboard."

—Meriwether Lewis
May 1805

In the confusion, some of the explorers' supplies washed out of the boat. The supplies included papers and guiding instruments. Sacagawea quickly scooped up the instruments and papers before they sank. Long Knife and Red Hair thanked Sacagawea for saving their possessions.

Timeline

Sacagawea began her journey with the **Corps** of Discovery	The explorers' boat overturned
April 7, 1805	May 1805

Sacagawea's Lemhi Shoshone childhood prepared her for traveling. She knew how to make a fire easily.

Danger Along the Way

In early June, traveling became impossible for Sacagawea. She had a bad fever. The group decided to camp until Sacagawea was well enough to continue. Sacagawea felt hot and weak. She thought she might die. Sacagawea worried about what would happen to Pomp if she did not get better.

In Their Own Words

"The Indian woman [is] extremely ill. . . This gave me some concern . . . for [her], then with a young child in her arms."

—Meriwether Lewis
June 16, 1805

After several days, Lewis brought Sacagawea
a drink of special water from a nearby **spring**.
By the next day, Sacagawea felt much better.
She was grateful to Lewis. But within hours,
Sacagawea's fever returned. After a day or two,
she felt better. Sacagawea was well enough to
travel again.

*Lewis thought that water from the spring
would help Sacagawea feel better.*

On June 29th, the group came to the Great Falls of the Missouri River. They climbed a hill to look at the beautiful waterfall. Lewis and Clark decided it was time to head back to camp. Suddenly, the sky turned black. Heavy rains began to fall. Clark, Sacagawea, Pomp, and Charbonneau took **shelter** under a cliff.

Photographer F. Jay Haynes took this photograph of the Great Falls in 1880.

Water began to rise around their feet. In a few minutes, the water had risen to their knees. Clark climbed to the top of the cliff. He reached down to Sacagawea. Sacagawea lifted Pomp up to Clark. The water was now at Sacagawea's waist. She struggled to keep from being carried away. Clark then pulled Sacagawea and Charbonneau to safety. Sacagawea was grateful to Lewis and Clark. She began to think of them as friends.

This painting of the rainstorm at Great Falls is by artist Olaf C. Selzer.

A Happy Reunion

In August of 1805 Sacagawea began to recognize the forests and rivers. The group was traveling through areas where the Lemhi Shoshones hunted. One night the group camped near the Jefferson River. Sacagawea could see the place where she had been **kidnapped** as a girl. She knew her **homeland** was nearby. On August 17th several American Indian men rode horses toward the explorers. Sacagawea recognized them as Lemhi Shoshone, her own **tribe.**

In Their Own Words

"Sacagawea . . . began to dance and show . . . the most **extravagant** joy."

—William Clark
August 17, 1805

Sacagawea was so excited that she began to jump with joy. She told Charbonneau that these men were from her tribe. When the men came closer, Sacagawea shouted to them. She told them that the explorers came in peace. The Lemhi Shoshone men invited the group to their camp.

This photograph of Shoshone men on horseback was taken around 1900.

*Sacagawea did not recognize Cameahwait until she started **interpreting**.*

At the camp Sacagawea followed Lewis and Clark into the chief's tent. The voice of the chief sounded familiar to Sacagawea. She looked at him closely. The man was her brother, Cameahwait. Sacagawea and her brother talked about her family. She learned that her father had died shortly after the Hidatsa attack. Her sister, Pine Girl, also had died. Sacagawea cried when she heard this news.

Sacagawea told Cameahwait that the explorers were drawing a map for traders. The traders would bring guns and blankets to the Lemhi Shoshones. She hoped Cameahwait would give the group horses to cross the mountains. Cameahwait agreed. The group stayed with the Lemhi Shoshones for two weeks. Sacagawea then said good-bye to her family and friends. She told her brother that she had to go with the explorers. She wanted to help them reach the "big water."

*This painting shows the **Corps** of Discovery crossing the Bitterroot Mountains after leaving the Lemhi Shoshone camp. It was painted by John Clymer.*

At the Pacific Ocean

The group reached the Oregon coast by December of 1805. They built a winter camp called Fort Clatsop. The following spring Sacagawea, Charbonneau, and

Pomp returned home to the Hidatsa village. In 1809 the whole family moved to St. Louis, Missouri. Two years later, Sacagawea and Charbonneau returned to the West. They left Pomp with William Clark in St. Louis. Sacagawea thought Pomp would have a good life there.

Timeline

Corps of Discovery reached the Pacific Ocean	Sacagawea's family returned to the Hidatsa village	Sacagawea and Charbonneau took Pomp to live with Clark	Sacagawea and Charbonneau moved to Fort Manuel	Sacagawea gave birth to Lisette. Sacagawea died on December 20
December 1805	**1806**	**1809**	**1811**	**1812**

It took the Corps of Discovery about three weeks to build Fort Clatsop.

Sacagawea and Charbonneau went to live at Fort Manuel in present-day South Dakota. There Charbonneau worked as a trader. Sacagawea had a daughter, Lisette, in 1812. Soon Sacagawea became sick. She died on December 20th at the age of 24. Some people believe that the woman who died at Fort Manuel was actually Mountain Sage, not Sacagawea. They say Sacagawea moved to a Shoshone **reservation** in Wyoming. They believe Sacagawea died in 1884. Most Lemhi Shoshones do not accept this.

A Woman of Courage

Today, people remember Sacagawea as a brave woman. She was taken from her family as a girl. As a young mother, she traveled many miles to help serve an important **mission.** People have built several monuments in Sacagawea's honor. One monument is in Mobridge, South Dakota, near the Missouri River. Another bronze statue stands at the Sacajawea Cultural Interpretive Center near Salmon, Idaho.

This statue of Sacagawea was made by artist Leonard Crunelle in 1910. It is located near the state capitol building in Bismarck, North Dakota.

No images were made of Sacagawea during her lifetime. However, the artist who designed the coin used an American Indian woman as a model.

In 2000 the United States **Mint** released a new dollar coin in memory of Sacagawea. The golden dollar coin features Sacagawea with Pomp strapped to her back. Sacagawea's story continues to be an **inspiration** to people. She stands out in history as a **symbol** of peace and strength.

Glossary

anxious feeling of looking forward to something

corps organized part of a country's military

dome round roof that is shaped like the top half of a globe

extravagant showing something to extreme measures

hide skin of a large, dead animal, usually with the fur still on it

homeland place that a person comes from

inspiration person, thing, or idea that makes people excited about doing something

interpret translate one language into another

kidnap steal a person

mint place where metals are made into coins

mission special or important job

nomadic people who always move from place to place

puzzled   confused by something that does not make sense

reconstruct   build again

reservation   land kept by Indians when they signed treaties

shelter   protection from the weather

spring   place where water comes out of the ground

symbol   something that stands for something else

translate   change words from one language to another

tribe   group of people who share language, customs, beliefs, and often government

warrior   person who fights in battles

More Books to Read

Alter, Judy. *Sacagawea: Native American Interpreter.* Eden Prairie, Minn.: Child's World, 2002.

Ditchfield, Christin. *The Shoshone.* Danbury, Conn.: Scholastic Library, 2003.

Stout, Mary. *Lewis and Clark.* Chicago: Raintree, 2003.

Index